T0197424

The Extraordinary Story of Christmas

Mary, Joseph and the
Birth of Jesus

Jo Collins

WestBow Press books may be ordered through booksellers or by contacting:

WestBow Press
A Division of Thomas Nelson & Zondervan
1663 Liberty Drive
Bloomington, IN 47403
www.westbowpress.com
844-714-3454

ISBN: 978-1-6642-6199-0 (sc)
ISBN: 978-1-6642-6200-3 (e)

Library of Congress Control Number: 2022905741

Print information available on the last page.

WestBow Press rev. date: 06/28/2022

WESTBOW
P R E S S®
A DIVISION OF THOMAS NELSON
& ZONDERVAN

The Extraordinary Story
of Christmas

CHAPTER ONE
Mary's Parents Pray for a Baby

———◆•◈•◆———

Mary's mother and father had been married for many years and had not been able to have children. This made them very sad. The older they got the sadder they became. They wanted a baby so much that they prayed to God and asked Him to make that happen! They promised God, if He would answer their prayers and give them a child, they would dedicate their baby to Him.[1]

Mary's father was a scroll scholar which meant he studied the Old Testament Bible. He worked in a synagogue, or what was their church, in a town by the name of Sepphoris.[2] Sepphoris was not far from Nazareth where they all lived. Because he was a scroll scholar he knew all the verses in the Bible. Included in the Bible were some very important ones about the birth of a child who would grow up and become the savior of the world. Even though they were both familiar with these verses, Mary's parents had no idea when they prayed for a baby, that these verses were part of their prayer.

They both promised God that if He gave them a baby, they would raise their child to love Him. Little did they know that God had been waiting for both of them to promise this! God immediately answered their prayer with a cute baby girl! They named her Mary.

CHAPTER TWO
Why the Name Mary?

———◆———

There are times in history when one name is more popular than others. The name Mary was very popular back then because of a well-known story in the Old Testament about a man named Moses who saved the Jewish people from slavery. He had a sister named Mary (which is pronounced Miriam in the Old Testament). Many parents picked the name Mary, for their babies, because they loved the stories about Moses and his sister.[3] Moses was famous because he led millions of people out of Egypt where they had been slaves. His sister Mary helped him do this. But perhaps more important than that, when Moses was a little baby and Mary a young girl, she helped save his life. It was because of his sister's bravery that his life was spared. Without her, Moses would not have lived long enough to be anyone famous!

All this happened because at the time Moses was born, King Pharaoh had issued an order commanding all Jewish midwives to kill every baby boy as soon as he was born. A midwife was a woman trained like a nurse to deliver a baby. If a midwife did not kill the baby boy, then one of Pharaoh's soldiers would. The midwives knew this was wrong and they refused to do this terrible thing. Moses' parents kept his birth a secret and hid him as long as they could. Finally he was too active to hide any longer. Moses' mother had to come up with a plan to keep her baby safe before the soldiers could find him. She prayed to God and He showed her what she should do. She made a little baby bed for him that would float. Not too far down the river, the daughter of Pharaoh and her servants were taking a bath. She placed Moses in his little floating bed and down the river he floated to the exact spot where Pharaoh's daughter was bathing.

Miriam or "Mary" ran along the river and followed her baby brother. When Pharaoh's daughter retrieved the floating basket and saw the baby, she fell in love with Moses. Mary bravely stepped forward and spoke to the princess! Mary asked her if she needed a nurse for the baby. And of course she did! Mary explained that her mother could take care of the baby until the baby was old enough to live with the princess at the palace. The plan worked! Her brother was now safe and got to go home and live with his family until he was weened.[4]

It was because of this story from the Old Testament about the sister of Moses, that Mary's parents choose the name Mary for her! It proved to be the perfect name. Their own little Mary would one day grow up to be the mother of a son who would save the whole world from the slavery of sin. Just like Mary from the Old Testament, she would have to be very brave to do this!

CHAPTER THREE

Mary Grows Up

Mary's parents kept their promise to God. As soon as their baby was born, they dedicated her life to Him. As Mary grew up, they taught her all about God and how to love Him. They told her that her birth was a miracle from Him and an answer to their prayer. Deep down on the inside she believed that she was born for a special purpose. As she grew up she kept these things in her heart. She loved going to the synagogue. She loved learning about God. She loved to pray and worship. Each day she used her talents and abilities to honor Him in all she did. She grew in favor with both God and people.[5]

When Mary was about 14 years old, her dad was contacted by the father of a handsome young man named Joseph. Joseph was ready to be married and his parents were looking for a wife for their son. At that time, marriages were arranged by parents for their children.[6] It seems strange to us today, but parents did not leave such an important thing to chance! A father of a young woman wanted to protect his daughter from marrying anyone who would not take good care of her. A father of a young man wanted his son to find and marry a loving, caring wife who would work together with their son to create a nice home to raise a family. Establishing a strong, loving family was very important.

Joseph's father was a craftsman. A craftsman was a person highly skilled in working with wood and stone.[7] Today we might say he was a master craftsman and in charge of getting places built! His family may have been one of the wealthiest families in Nazareth! His son, Joseph was also becoming a master craftsman! Joseph and his father would most likely have had lots of work. This was important because Joseph would be able to build a beautiful home and earn a good income for

Mary and their future family. Mary's parents knew that this young man, Joseph, would be an excellent husband for Mary. Not only did he have a good job, he was a fine young Jewish man who kept all the commandments of God. He seemed to be the perfect match for their miracle daughter. Together they would love God and serve Him.

CHAPTER FOUR

Mary and Joseph Betrothed

————◆————

In fact, both sets of parents thought their children were a perfect match for each other! So Mary and Joseph were betrothed. Being betrothed was a promise to marry. Betrothal lasted one full year! For the next twelve months they would have little or no contact with each other. During this time, Joseph and Mary and their families would stay busy making all the preparations for marriage. Mary was learning to be a good wife. Joseph and his father would stay busy building a house for them to live in to raise a family. Joseph and Mary promised to spend this time preparing for a lifelong commitment to one another. [8]

But before that year of preparation was over, Mary had an experience that would change everything! It changed not only her life but the destiny of the entire world! It began with a visit from God's angel Gabriel! He appeared to Mary and spoke with her. We can read what Gabriel told her in the Bible in Luke 1:30-33. He told Mary, "Don't be afraid! God is pleased with you, and you will have a son. His name will be Jesus. He will be great and will be called the Son of God Most High. The Lord God will make him king, as his ancestor David was. He will rule the people of Israel forever, and his kingdom will never end." (Contemporary English Version)

What the angel Gabriel told Mary was that she would soon become a mother and have a baby boy named Jesus! He said that her son, Jesus, would be God's son and would become a King! Gabriel said the Kingdom belonging to Jesus would last forever and ever! It would never end. Mary knew this meant King Jesus would also be the Savior of the world. She knew this because it was written in the Old Testament Bible. Her mother and father had taught her those very scriptures from the time that she was born. She understood exactly what the angel Gabriel was telling her. Now she knew her special purpose. Her assignment from God was to give birth to His son who would be the Savior of the world. What Mary didn't understand was how would this be able to happen? The angel Gabriel answered her question. He said, "The Holy Spirit will come upon you, and the power of the Highest will overshadow you. Therefore the Holy One who will be born will be called the Son of God." (Luke 1:35 Modern English Version) The angel Gabriel explained that everything would happen by the supernatural power of God! She need not worry about it or be afraid! Mary replied, "I am the Lord's servant. Let it be with me just as you have said." (Luke 1:38 Common English Bible)

The angel Gabriel also told her that her cousin Elizabeth was expecting a baby.[9] Mary knew Elizabeth had never been able to have children. This also had to be a miracle! God was able to do anything! Two miracle babies were going to be born! They would be cousins born six months apart. Elizabeth would name her baby boy John. Mary would name her baby boy Jesus. God, the one who always existed, who calls himself "I Am Who I Am"[10] was about to have a son born on the earth! He had chosen Mary to be the mother of His son, Jesus! She was excited about this, but she also had a reason to be concerned.

CHAPTER FIVE

Joseph Stays with Mary

———◄•◆•►———

Mary had not forgotten that she was betrothed to Joseph. What would he say? She had promised to have his children and his only. How was she going to tell him? And would he believe her? This was not so good. There was even a law that stated that a woman could be punished with death because of this! Mary decided it best to go visit and stay with her cousin Elizabeth for a little while. Even with her gone, it did not take very long before Joseph found out!

When he learned that Mary was having a baby, he was more than a little upset. But upset as he was, he did not want to see her hurt or punished for it. He truly loved Mary! Even though Joseph loved her, he decided it would be best not to marry her. He decided to privately and secretly send her away. After all, she was already at her Cousin Elizabeth's house. But that was not part of God's plan! He wanted Joseph to be a husband to Mary and be the stepfather to His son. God had to explain this to Joseph. Right away, He sent an angel to tell Joseph in a dream to stay betrothed to Mary.[11] The angel was able to calm all his fears and assure him that this was God's plan for both of them. The angel told Joseph to stay with Mary. And he did. Joseph agreed to raise Mary's baby and be the best stepfather he could to God's son. Joseph knew that this baby boy would grow into a man who would one day die to save all people from their sins. Joseph had read about this in the Old Testament Bible. The Jewish people, including Joseph, himself, had been waiting, watching and wondering when this would happen. So Joseph took Mary to be his wife. Now together both of them were anxiously awaiting the birth of a son. God's son, baby Jesus!

CHAPTER SIX

Travel to Bethlehem

——◆——

Right before the due date for Jesus to be born, Caesar Augustus made a decree that every man had to return to his hometown where he had been born. Each man had to sign a register and show how many were now in the family. It was called a census. Caesar Augustus did this because he wanted to know how many people lived in his Kingdom. Once the people were all counted, Caesar Augustus would know how much money he would collect in taxes. By this time, Mary and Joseph were all ready for the baby to be born. It would have been much better to stay put, but they had no choice but to make the journey back to Joseph's home town of Bethlehem. It was dangerous to travel that far so late in her pregnancy, but Mary knew God would take care of her and the baby. They packed what they needed on donkeys and made the journey to Bethlehem for the census.

The town had not changed much since Joseph had left. But when they arrived, it was packed with people! In fact, there were so many people there was no place for Joseph and Mary to stay. Normally, this was not a problem. They knew people in town they might stay with, but everyone had guests because of the census. Most of the homes in Bethlehem had a flat roof with a guestroom on the roof for visitors. When more rooms were needed, the area next to a house, where a family keep their donkey or goat, was cleaned and used for a guestroom. Because of the census, even all of these rooms were full! Joseph and Mary began wondering where they would find a place to stay. They had camped out each night on the journey to get there and it looked like they would have to camp out in Bethlehem also. They had passed by several caves outside of town. These caves were used by shepherds who were out tending to their sheep. A cave was not the best place for a baby to be born, but it was safe and dry and they could make due.[12] They knew God was watching over them!

Joseph and Mary had travelled for about ten days just to get to Bethlehem and they were very tired. The long journey walking and riding a donkey was strenuous for Mary. Strenuous enough to start labor but baby Jesus waited until they had everything set up inside the cave. Joseph immediately asked where he could find a midwife to help with the birth of the baby.[13] As soon as they had everything ready, Mary went into labor. What they had been waiting for was about to happen!

CHAPTER SEVEN

Jesus is Born

With her husband Joseph by her side and the midwife helping her, Mary went through her labor pains and gave birth to baby Jesus. Mary and Joseph felt the presence and love of God as the baby was born. Everyone in that cave could feel it and sense it. Jesus was a little baby on the outside, but on the inside was God. He was God's son and His eternal spirit had been placed inside of Him as soon as He had begun to grow inside of His mother. Now the Word that had been with God in the beginning and, in fact, was God and created everything with God, was now a baby boy. God's own son was born! The Word was now a baby named Jesus![14] Mary wrapped him in swaddling clothes to keep him warm and bundled up. Swaddling clothes were strips of cloth normally used on baby lambs to strengthen and protect their legs. But it worked well for wrapping baby Jesus and kept him feeling snuggled and warm. A feeding trough for sheep, called a manger, made a perfect little bed for him to sleep. There was a calm, peace and happiness inside that cave as Mary and Joseph admired and cared for their new baby boy. Little Jesus was safe, warm and loved! His start in life was very humble. Any other baby born that was this important would have been born in a palace! After all, baby Jesus was also God who would one day become an eternal King and save the world. The story of this humble birth had been written thousands of years earlier and it happened exactly the way it had been written.[15] God tells us what will happen ahead of time so we can look forward to it. Baby Jesus was sleeping in a manger for a reason. Swaddling clothes were used as his blanket for a reason. God was, in fact, letting the world know that Jesus was born innocent and sweet, much like a small baby lamb.

18

CHAPTER EIGHT

God Announces the Birth of His Son!

—•◆•—

God was ecstatic that His son Jesus was born! At that time, and even today, when someone important is born it is announced to everyone! God did announce it, but not to everyone. He sent one of His angels to make the announcement to a few shepherds who were keeping watch over their flock of sheep that night. These shepherds were the very first to hear that baby Jesus had been born! However, they were not your ordinary every day shepherds. They were shepherds on special assignment to take care of the lambs that would be killed in the temple. [16]

The temple was a place, like a church, where people came to worship and draw close to God. In fact, the very presence of God was in the temple! But there was sometimes a problem that prevented people from being able to draw close to God. God is perfect and when a person did something wrong or bad they could not be in His presence. They were not able to go to the temple. So, God had to set up a way for people to be able to draw near to Him even when they sinned or did bad things. It was a very hard lesson to learn! A lamb had to die so that the guilty person could be free from the consequence of not being with God.[17] The person giving up the lamb was very sorry for what he or she had done wrong and did not want to do it again! Some of the meat from the lamb was given to families for their food.[18] It was a severe penalty but God did not want sin to separate Him from His people. He loves everyone so much that He sent His only son, Jesus, that whoever believes in His son would be able to stay close to God for always.

The Bible tells us exactly what happened the night when the angel visited the shepherds. "The angel of the Lord came upon them, and the glory of the Lord shone round about them; and they were sore afraid. And the angel said unto them, fear not; for, behold, I bring you good tidings of great joy, which shall be to all people. For unto you is born this day in the city of David a Savior, which is Christ the Lord. And this shall be a sign unto you; ye shall find the babe wrapped in swaddling clothes, lying in a manger. And suddenly there was with the angel a multitude of the heavenly host praising God, and saying, glory to God in the highest, and on earth peace, good will toward men." (Luke 2:9-14 King James Version)

The shepherds were shocked and afraid! The glory of the Lord was there which meant the presence and power of God was there! In fact it shone all around them like a brilliant light! This was unlike anything they had ever seen or felt before! And an angel of God talked directly to them. Not only that, they witnessed a whole army of angels praising God![19] These were in fact God's fighting angels on patrol that night. Not only were they guarding and watching over baby Jesus and his family, they were also praising God for the birth of the commander of their army. Their job was to protect Jesus and to obey Him. No harm would come to Jesus that night! Or any other night until Jesus' time on earth and his job was finished! What an amazing encounter! The shepherds were overcome with joy and a desire to go see this baby who the Angel called Christ the Lord. No way would they be able to sleep that night!

CHAPTER NINE

Shepherds Worship the Lamb

———— ◆◆◆ ————

As soon as the army of angels dispersed, the shepherds left to find baby Jesus. They knew where to look because the angel had given them two signs. One sign was a newborn baby lying in a manger. The other sign was a newborn baby wrapped in swaddling clothes. They knew to look for a shepherds cave because that is where mangers and swaddling clothes were kept. And find baby Jesus they did! As soon as they entered the cave where he was born, a spirit of worship overcame them. It was like a heavy blanket had fallen on them. They immediately bowed down before their newborn King and began to worship Him! Tears came and they did not usually cry! They told Mary and Joseph everything that had happened that night. They repeated what the angel had said, "behold, I bring you good tidings of great joy, which shall be to all people. For unto you is born this day in the city of David a Savior, which is Christ the Lord. And this shall be a sign unto you; ye shall find the babe wrapped in swaddling clothes, lying in a manger." (Luke 2:10-12 King James Version)

The shepherds were happy to be with Joseph, Mary and baby Jesus! And both Mary and Joseph were happy to see the shepherds and hear about the angels! Even baby Jesus was happy and smiled at them. The shepherds knew without any doubt that Jesus was God' son. They were also beginning to understand that Jesus would be like the little lambs they had been taking care of in the field that night.[20] Those lambs had to be perfect. That was why they put the swaddling clothes on the baby lambs so they would not have cuts, hurts or scars on their legs. Jesus would have to grow up and live a perfect life. And He did. He was full of God's love! He never did anything wrong or bad. He never sinned. Like those lambs who died in the temple, Jesus would one day die so every man, woman and child could always be with God. God sent his only son, Jesus so that everyone who believes in Him can live with God forever.[21]

The next day the shepherds told everyone they met what they had seen and heard that night! The good news began to spread that the Lamb of God, God's own son, the Savior of the world, the King without end, baby Jesus had been born.

Prayer

Dear God,

I know that I have sinned and I have thought and acted badly. Thank you for having your son, Jesus, born on the earth for me. Thank you Jesus for being like a little lamb and dying so I can be forgiven. Thank you God for raising Jesus' body from the grave. Thank you God and Jesus for doing all these things so I can live with both of you forever. Jesus, please come into my life and my heart and help me not to sin any more. I want to follow you and live my life for you. God, help me to receive everything that you want me to have so I can become like Jesus.

(If you pray this prayer out loud to God and Jesus and believe it in your heart, then you are saved and will have eternal life.)

About the Illustrator

Ambur Byler is a sixteen year-old homeschooled student and illustrator. In her free time, she enjoys teaching herself various styles of art and techniques. She loves country life and morning coffee on her family's ranch in Missouri.

About the Author

———◆·◆·◆———

Jo Collins is a licensed minister with Assemblies of God Fellowship and has a degree in Human Services, Counseling. She loves teaching from the Bible and strives to be a standard bearer of God's word. For over 30 years she has been teaching Bibles studies to every age group and serving others through various non-profit organizations and Christian ministries. She was instrumental in reorganizing and running a women's domestic violence program for seven years and is currently a co-founder of a non-profit which help women overcome obstacles related to drug use. She is passionate about being a doer of God's word and not a hearer only. She lives with her husband and they split their time between their city and country home. They enjoy travel and spending time with their families.

Endnotes

1   Renner, Rick. *Christmas: the rest of the story. 15-Part Audio Series.* (Copyright 2019) [CD-Rom] Produced by Rick Renner Ministries. Available at renner.org.

2   Renner, Rick. *Christmas: the rest of the story. 15-Part Audio Series.* (Copyright 2019) [CD-Rom] Produced by Rick Renner Ministries. Available at renner.org.

3   The name Miriam or "Mary" was popular in the first century among the Jewish people because of the story of Miriam in the Old Testament. "Mary." *The meaning of the name.com/Mary.* Published by 2020The meaning of the name. Copyright 2020. History and origin, paragraph nine. www.themeaningofthename/ mary.com. Accessed information May 7, 2020.

4   Exodus 2:2-10 (New King James Version) So the woman conceived and bore a son. And when she saw that he *was* a beautiful *child,* she hid him three months. [3] But when she could no longer hide him, she took an ark of bulrushes for him, daubed it with asphalt and pitch, put the child in it, and laid *it* in the reeds by the river's bank. [4] And his sister stood afar off, to know what would be done to him. [5] Then the daughter of Pharaoh came down to bathe at the river. And her maidens walked along the riverside; and when she saw the ark among the reeds, she sent her maid to get it. [6] And when she opened *it,* she saw the child, and behold, the baby wept. So she had compassion on him, and said, "This is one of the Hebrews' children." [7] Then his sister said to Pharaoh's daughter, "Shall I go and call a nurse for you from the Hebrew women, that she may nurse the child for you?" [8] And Pharaoh's daughter said to her, "Go." So the maiden went and called the child's mother. [9] Then Pharaoh's daughter said to her, "Take this child away and nurse him for me, and I will give *you* your wages." So the woman took the child and nursed him.

5   Luke 1:28 (New King James Version.) "And having come in, the angel said to her, Rejoice, highly favored *one,* the Lord *is* with you; blessed *are* you among women!"

6   Marriages were arranged by the parents. The average age for a girl to marry was between 12 and 14 years of age. Renner, Rick, *Christmas, the rest of the story. Companion study guide.* Tulsa Oklahoma. Published by Rick Renner Ministries. Copyright 2019.

7   Carpenter means to be an artificer. Young, Robert. (1964, 1969, 1970). Carpenter. *Young's Analytical concordance to the bible.* (p. 144). WM. B. Eerdmans Publishing Company. According to *Webster's New Universal Unabridged Dictionary,* Artificer is a "skillful or artistic worker; craftsman." Artificer. (1989) *Webster's new universal unabridged dictionary.* Barnes and Noble.

8   Renner, Rick, *Christmas: the rest of the story, companion study guide.* Tulsa, Oklahoma. Published by Rick Renner Ministries. Copyright 2019.

9   Luke 1:36 (New King James Version). Now indeed, Elizabeth your relative has also conceived a son in her old age; and this is now the sixth month for her who was called barren.

10 Exodus 3:14 (The Book of Yahweh, the Holy Scriptures Translation). Then Yahweh said to Mosheh: I am Who I am. And He said: This is what you are to say to The children of Israyol; YAHWEH has sent me to you. "I Am" means "to happen, come to pass, occur, to exist, be in existence, to abide, remain, continue" etc. Blue letter bible interlinear concordance online. Host. www.blueletterbible.org. accessed May 7, 2020.

11 Matthew 1:20 (New King James Version). But while he thought about these things, behold, an angel of the Lord appeared to him in a dream, saying, "Joseph, son of David, do not be afraid to take to you Mary your wife, for that which is conceived in her is of the Holy Spirit.

12 Most Christmas stories place the birth of Jesus in a barn or stable, however this is not historically correct. Early writers place Jesus's birth in a cave. Renner, Rick. *Christmas: the rest of the story.* 15-Part Audio Series. (Copyright 2019) [CD-Rom] Produced by Rick Renner Ministries. Available at renner.org.

13 It was common practice for a midwife to be present at all Jewish births, especially for a first time mother. Harmon, Patricia. "Was there a midwife at the manger? Here's what the history of childbirth says about the first Christmas." *Time.com/5481431/birth-of-Jesus-midwife-history-Christmas, TIME trust in.* Time USA, LLC. December 19, 2018. Accessed May 7, 2020.

14 John 1:14 (New King James Version). And the Word became flesh and dwelt among us, and we beheld His glory, the glory as of the only begotten of the Father, full of grace and truth.

15 The prophet Isaiah in the Old Testament foretold of the birth of Jesus in Isaiah 1:9 (New King James Version) For unto us a Child is born, Unto us a Son is given; And the government will be upon His shoulder. And His name will be called Wonderful, Counselor, Mighty God, Everlasting Father, Prince of Peace.

16 Renner, Rick. *Christmas: the rest of the story.* 15-Part Audio Series. (Copyright 2019) [CD-Rom] Produced by Rick Renner Ministries. Available at renner.org.

17 Leviticus 4:35 (New King James Version). He shall remove all its fat, as the fat of the lamb is removed from the sacrifice of the peace offering. Then the priest shall burn it on the altar, according to the offerings made by fire to the Lord. So the priest shall make atonement for his sin that he has committed, and it shall be forgiven him.

18 Numbers 18:9-10 (New King James Version) This shall be yours of the most holy things *reserved* from the fire: every offering of theirs, every grain offering and every sin offering and every trespass offering which they render to Me, *shall be* most holy for you and your sons. [10] In a most holy *place* you shall eat it; every male shall eat it. It shall be holy to you.

19 Heavenly Hosts refers to God's army of angels. Blue letter bible interlinear concordance online. Host. www.blueletterbible.org. Accessed May 7, 2020.

20 Jesus is referred to as a Lamb in both the Old and New Testament. In the Old Testament in Isaiah 53:7 (New King James Version) He was oppressed and He was afflicted, Yet He opened not His mouth; He was led as a lamb to the slaughter, And as a sheep before its shearers is silent, So He opened not His mouth. In the New Testament in John 1:36 (New King James Version) And looking at Jesus as He walked, he said, "Behold the Lamb of God!"

21 John 3:16 (New King James Version) For God so loved the world that He gave His only begotten Son, that whoever believes in Him should not perish but have everlasting life.

Printed in the United States
by Baker & Taylor Publisher Services